The Spring of My Life

THE SPRING OF MY LIFE

And Selected Haiku
by Kobayashi Issa

Translated from the Japanese by
Sam Hamill

Illustrated by Kaji Aso

SHAMBHALA
Boston & London
1997

Shambhala Publications, Inc.
Horticultural Hall
300 Massachusetts Avenue
Boston, Massachusetts 02115
http://www.shambhala.com

© 1997 by Sam Hamill

Illustrations © 1997 by Kaji Aso

Portions of this book have been published previously in *The American Poetry Review*, *Shenandoah*, and *Five Points*. Some of the haiku was included in *The Sound of Water: Haiku by Bashō, Buson, Issa and Others* (Shambhala Publications, 1995). Several haiku have been revised for this edition.

⊗ This edition is printed on acid-free paper that meets the American National Standards Institute z39.48 Standard.

Distributed in the United States by Random House, Inc., and in Canada by Random House of Canada Ltd

Library of Congress Cataloging-in-Publications Data
Kobayashi, Issa, 1763-1827.
Spring of my life and selected haiku/by Kobayashi Issa; translated by Sam Hamill.
p.   cm.
ISBN 1-57062-144-6 (pbk.: alk. paper)
1. Kobayashi, Issa, d1763-1827—Translations into English.
I. Hamill, Sam.   II. Title.
PL797.2.A24   1997   97-7530
895.6'134—dc21   CIP

For Hayden Carruth and Denise Levertov
And for Brother Yusuke

Contents

Translator's Introduction

Kobayashi Yatarō, revered throughout the world as Issa, which means One Cup of Tea, was born in 1763 on a farm in Kashiwabara village in central Japan, now Nagano Prefecture. The surrounding mountains of his beloved Shinano countryside are eternally associated with his name, just as the mountainous north country made famous by Bashō's *Narrow Road to the Interior* is often referred to as "Bashō country."

But it is Issa's unfortunate life much more than the landscape that has made him such an endearing figure. He spent most of his life obsessed with a sense of loss, exiled from his home by a stepmother so repugnant as to seem almost lifted from a fairy tale. His poverty during adulthood was so profound that he often had no home at all, sleeping at the homes of friends or students and calling himself Issa the Beggar.

And yet his poems reveal an abiding love for suffering humanity, even for animals, insects, and plants, a devoutly Buddhist spiritual compassion.

Fly, butterfly!
I feel the dust of this world
weighting my body!

Issa's poems about animals and insects are learned by
every schoolchild in Japan, and almost everyone can
recite a few of his poems on occasion. Writing poetry
was a fundamental part of his spiritual practice, and he
wrote with dedication, producing more than twenty
thousand haiku, hundreds of tanka, and several works
of *haibun*, a combination of poetic prose and haiku.

Under shady trees,
sharing space with a butterfly—
this, too, is karma

Issa never dwelled long on karma, although he must
have felt that he'd sown some ugly seeds in some previ-
ous incarnation. Shortly after his second birthday, his
mother died. He was sent to be raised by his grand-
mother, who provided for his study with a local haiku
poet, Shimpo, to begin his education. When Issa was
seven, his father remarried. Near his tenth birthday, his
stepmother gave birth to a son. No one will ever know
exactly what transpired thereafter, but years later Issa
wrote that his clothes were "perpetually soaked with
urine from the baby" and that he was beaten "a hundred

times a day." Whenever the baby cried, Issa was blamed and beaten. He claimed to have spent nights weeping at Myōsen Temple. Finding refuge there undoubtedly had a profound effect on the boy.

He was sent to work in the fields, and his studies with Shimpo ended. When Issa was thirteen, his beloved grandmother died. His father, thinking to ease familial antagonism and suffering, sent the young poet to apprentice himself to a literary man in Edo (now Tokyo) who offered lodging in exchange for copy work. However, Issa never made use of the letter of introduction. He disappeared into busy city life, and no record of these years exists. He may have worked as a clerk at a Buddhist temple.

> So much money made
> by clever temple priests
> using peonies

Years later, Issa would write that he often lived hungry, cold, and homeless in Edo.

By the late 1880s, Issa's name began to appear in association with a group of haiku poets studying under Chikua, who followed in the "Bashō tradition," cultivating a plain, direct style steeped in the broth of Zen. A hundred years earlier, Bashō had single-handedly elevated haiku from a form of intellectual poetic exercise to high art. He advocated the Way of Poetry (*kadō*) as an alternative to the values of the emerging merchant class, also following a Way of Elegance (*fuga no michi*), claiming that his life was "stitched together by a single thread of art." Bashō felt bound by "neither religious law nor popular custom," but sought through haiku and *haibun* to "follow in the footsteps of the masters" of classical Chinese poetry and Zen. It is said that Bashō always carried a copy of the Taoist text *Chuang Tzu* and that this pre-Zen spiritual classic flavors his poetry with *mono no aware*, a sense of beauty intensified by recognition of temporality, and *sabi*, a kind of spiritual loneliness. Chuang Tzu's lively sense of humor is also reflected in many of Bashō's verses.

The qualities of *mono no aware* and *sabi* are everywhere evident in Issa's poetry; *sabi* is derived from *sabishi*, meaning "loneliness," a word he used again and again. His early haiku often reveal the profound influence of Bashō despite sometimes slipping into self-pity. Issa, like Bashō, went to school on the poetry of the great poet-monk Saigyō, who brought the distinct flavor of Zen to Japanese "nature poetry" in the twelfth century. Issa's own unique voice emerged fully only after years of daily practice and a profound assimilation of Buddhist ethics and poetry classics.

In early 1792, at age twenty-nine, he vowed to follow the Way of Poetry. He gave up the name Yatarō, and "began the new year anew" as Issa, living the life of a solitary sojourner for ten years as he explored Japan from its southern tip and eastern islands to the western Sea of Japan. Taking Bashō's *Narrow Road to the Interior* as a model, he traveled not for recreation or to find a tourist's view of his world, but to find himself. Issa the Beggar was born in the conviction that poetry can be a path to enlightenment. He believed that one part of that path is *shikan*, a meditative state in which perception is utterly free of discrimination between mind and matter, self and object; where the only permanence is impermanence and change, whether subtle or violent, remains the essence of being.

> Just being alive!
> —miraculous to be in
> cherry blossom shadows!

The cherry blossom in classical Japanese poetry represents much more than the beauty of the blossoms themselves. Because of the brevity of its life, a cherry blossom is a supreme figure of *mono no aware*, its beauty intensified because of its temporality. All great Japanese poems about cherry blossoms express a tinge of sadness, usually indirectly. "Just being alive!" may celebrate the beauty of the day, of the moment, but the blossoms suggest that life is brief and that we, too, shall soon disappear.

> Loneliness already
> planted with each seed in
> morning glory beds

"*Haya sabishi* (the loneliness is already there)," Issa says. There is loneliness in the first act, in the seed itself. Death and life are present in a cherry seed or morning glory seed and within the wandering poet. An old Zen proverb suggests "Live as though you were already dead!" The seed of death and the seed of life are one.

In the haiku tradition, the poem springs from attentive observation of ordinary life. Issa was a master at revealing the unsayable dimensions of the mundane, his poems always somehow conveying more than what the words alone suggest.

> Simply for all this,
> as if there were nothing else,
> heavy wet spring frost

In the hands of a lesser poet, this poem would drown in pseudoprofundity. Issa's gift is representative simplicity: "Simply for all this." There is no placement of detailed landscape. Issa enters the world of frost. It is almost rice-planting time, a task Bashō called "the beginning of culture." The spring calls forth ancient traditions and labors and all their consequences. It represents an end to winter, and by the lunar calendar, a beginning of a new year. Issa's restraint allows for complex evocation while acknowledging that utter simplicity underlies it all.

Issa was not the least bit reluctant to engage his imagination to manipulate circumstances to benefit his work. In *The Spring of My Life (Oraga haru)*, he presented what would become one of his most famous haiku as having been composed upon the death of his daughter:

> This world of dew
> is only the world of dew—
> and yet . . . oh and yet . . .

> *Tsuyu no yo wa*
> *tsuyu no yo nagara*
> *sarinagara*

Nobuyuki Yuasa points out in his 1960 translation of *Oraga haru* that this poem actually was composed earlier, upon the death of Issa's firstborn son. Whether Issa found no voice in direct response to his daughter's death or whether he simply thought the previous poem said it best doesn't really matter. Issa attributed the poem in a way that best suited the work in progress. In this, too, he followed Bashō's example.

Subject to the severe mood swings and almost constant undertone of melancholy that are a signature of abused children, Issa found both a spiritual path and a source of emotional stability in following the Way of Haiku. *The Spring of My Life,* his most famous work, represents a single year chosen almost at random, but is inspired and shaped by all of a fully lived life. This magnum opus is not just a notebook and an anthology, but also a testament and a sanctuary. Perhaps the most literal translation of the title would be simply "My New Spring," but while *haru* indeed means *spring,* in Japanese vernacular it refers to the New Year. On the lunar calendar, the first day of spring and the New Year often coincide.

Like Bashō, Issa did not settle immediately on the pen name by which he is known today. Earlier names included "Kobayashi Ikyo" and "Nirokuan Kikumei." Although he showed great promise at an early age, he was not satisfied for settling for mere popularity, and in 1792, he adopted the nom-de-plume Haikai-ji Nyudo Issa-bo, Temple of Haiku Lay Brother Issa.

> With spring's arrival,
> Yatarō becomes reborn
> as Issabo

> *Haru tatsuya*
> *Yatarō aratame*
> *Issabo*

He explained to a friend that his choice was inspired by a single bubble in a cup of tea rather than the tea itself, as the name would ordinarily suggest. He was not particularly fond of the tea ceremony as such, but felt that, like the bubble, our lives are brief and transparent. That poetry in general and haiku in particular indeed became his temple, and he a lay monk in its service, is beyond doubt. He took his vows seriously, and from that day on he lived a life of commitment.

Issa spent the following five or six years wandering throughout southern Japan, making "poetry friends" along the way. It was only after his return to Edo in 1778 that publication of his journals began to make him famous. Although less formally composed than *The Spring of My Life*, they reveal his deep study of Chinese poetry, anthologize many haiku and tanka by Japanese poets, and offer a view of Issa as a working poet who eagerly revised his poems, often leaving as many as six or seven "finished" versions of the same haiku.

In 1801, Issa's father was overcome with typhoid fever. Issa returned to Kashiwabara in time to nurse his father for a month before he finally succumbed. Issa's stepmother and stepbrother challenged his father's will, successfully depriving Issa of his inheritance for thirteen years. The poet wrote a poetic journal about his father's death, much of it marred by relentless, albeit understandable, sentimentality and self-pity.

For more than a decade, Issa lived in poverty, traveling back and forth between his native village and Edo, locked in a legal battle with his stepmother. These years weighed heavily on him. As he approached the age of fifty, he must have felt the family's internecine quarrels would never end. In 1810, he wrote:

> O moonlit blossoms—
> I've squandered forty-nine years
> walking beneath you

Finally, in 1813, negotiations with his family were completed and Issa returned to Kashiwabara. He married a young woman, and in 1816, she gave birth to a son who survived only a month. It was for this child that Issa wrote the "world of dew" poem. A daughter was born in 1818, only to died of smallpox a year later. It is this daughter, Sato, who is memorialized in *The Spring of My Life*, composed the following year.

Issa's life was plagued by sorrow. His second son, born in 1820, died several months after his birth. In 1822, a third son was born, but Issa's wife died painfully of illnesses related to arthritis shortly after his birth, and the boy died a few months later, in 1823, while in the care of an irresponsible nurse. During these years Issa also suffered failing health that resulted in periodic paralysis. In 1810, having temporarily lost his ability to speak, he had written:

> Such irritation!
> Even wandering wild geese
> can manage to speak

The poet recovered time and again from what may have been a series of small strokes, and married again in 1824, probably too soon, for this marriage dissolved in a matter of months. He had chosen for his new wife a woman from an esteemed local samurai family, and she apparently viewed his house and his ramshackle life with contempt, returning to her father's home after no more than a few weeks of marriage. Issa was overcome by some form of paralysis again while visiting Zenkō Temple and remained for a time in the care of a physician.

Seemingly undaunted, in 1826, at the age of sixty-four, he married for a third time. But the following year, his house caught fire and burned to the ground. Refusing offers to stay with students or friends, Issa and his pregnant wife moved into a tiny storehouse with neither windows nor stove, where they lived for several months. By all appearances, he seemed well on his way to overcoming this latest disaster when he died suddenly on November 19, 1827. His death prevented him from seeing the birth of his only surviving child, a daughter.

Two poems are attributed as Issa's last. One was found under his deathbed pillow:

> Gratitude for gifts,
> even snow on my bedspread
> a gift from the Pure Land

The other "death poem" may indeed be his last, especially if he deliberately placed the above, written earlier, as a final statement to be read following his death, which seems likely. The second poem:

> From birthing's washbowl
> to the washbowl of the dead—
> blathering nonsense!

Like so many of Issa's poems, this one invites several readings. Is the "blathering nonsense" the noisy busyness of suffering humanity and the world of desire, or has the poet come to a concluding caustic comment on his own life of letters? Is the poem an admonishment or a joke, a summation or a guffaw? Perhaps Issa had in mind the teaching of the *Samantabhadra Bodhisattva Sutra* that "the self is empty of independent existence," and all the "blathering nonsense" is the ambient noise of needless desire. Behind Issa's seemingly effortless simplicity, time and again, we find a complex universe.

If his life was shaped by intense feelings of exile and rejection, and punctuated by deep personal loss, it was shaped equally by remarkable courage and fearless conviction. In his day, as now, a monklike vow to live in the service of poetry was rare. Issa's faith in poetry as a path to enlightenment required living in accordance with what he had learned from noble old masters like Tu Fu, Po Chu-i, Saigyō, and Bashō. Issa paid no obeisance to rank, and roamed the streets of Edo in shabby robes, almost as famous for his behavior as for his verse. Once, summoned by a local daimyo, he was questioned about his art. Issa looked squarely into the eyes of the most dangerous man in the province and replied that he could not reduce his art to the level of dilettantes. Yet to most people he was a gentle eccentric. Children came to revere him as the poet-representative of small birds, bugs, and flowers.

Issa's poems reveal a deep engagement with the teachings of Zen, as well as with the Way of Haiku advocated by Bashō, and it is probably for these strengths of character, including his unabashed honesty, that he was admired by almost everyone regardless of social rank.

Japan has a long history of revering its poets—posthumously for the most part. There are many "Issa sites" and "haiku stones" with his poems engraved for posterity; his old homestead in Kashiwabara has been preserved. And, thanks to his only surviving child, his lineage continues.

In translating Issa's poems, I have held in my ear the sound of the original, the assonance and consonance, rhyme and slant rhyme that provides the foundation of the music of the original. Haiku grew out of the 5–7–5–7–7 syllabic structure of *waka* (later called tanka), which means simply "Japanese poem." Sounded out in the original, the "song" of haiku often includes a pregnant pause created by use of a "cutting word" (*kakekotoba*). Haiku was the first Japanese poetry (except that in the folk song tradition) to be written in the vernacular rather than in the highly refined language of the court. With its roots in the lyric tradition, it is meant to be heard.

Much of what passes for haiku, or the translation of haiku in American English, is not really either. Issa's poems have often been reduced to fragmentary English bearing little resemblance to the music, meaning or syntax of the original. I have sometimes made use of interpolation to fill out the music of these translations (American English tends to use fewer syllables than Japanese). But I have not made a Procrustean bed of syllabic structure. Sometimes a variation of a syllable or two suffices, especially when a long or heavy syllable is involved or when there is a sustained pause. My primary concern is to say what the poet says without rearranging the original order of perception.

Most of these poems are translated from *Issa Haikaishu* (Iwanami Shoten, 1990); others come from various sources, all checked for accuracy against the standard scholarly "complete works" *Issa Zenshu* (Shinamo Mainichi Shimbun-sha). Special thanks are due to my friend Keida Yusuke for his tireless efforts in helping "Obaka-san" bring the Japanese into Romaji (transliterated Japanese) and for his close reading of and helpful commentary on my translations. His generosity is evident on nearly every page. Nine bows.

SAM HAMILL
Kage-an, 1995-96

The Spring of My Life

ONE

Long ago, in Fuko Temple in Tango Province, there was a devout priest who made up his mind to celebrate New Year's Day to the fullest. So he wrote a letter on New Year's Eve, gave it to his novice with instructions to deliver it to him first thing the following morning, and sent him off to spend the night in the main hall.

With first light and the first crow caws, the novice rose in the long shadows and went to knock at the priest's door. He heard the priest's voice from deep within, asking who was calling. "A messenger," he replied, "sent from Amida, Buddha of the Pure Land, bearing seasonal greetings."

The door was thrust open and the still barefoot priest motioned his novice to take the seat of honor. He grabbed the letter and opened it quickly, reading aloud, "Give up the world of suffering! Come to the Pure Land. I will meet you along the way with a host of bodhisattvas!"

Tears rolled down the old priest's cheeks until they soaked his sleeves.

This story may at a glance seem terribly strange. After all, who would want to celebrate New Year's Day in sleeves soaked with tears, tears that were self-induced? Nevertheless, the priest's way was righteous: his principle duty was to bring the Buddha's teaching to this world. What better way to celebrate New Year's Day?

Still clothed in the dust of this suffering world, I celebrate the first day in my own way. And yet I am like the priest, for I too shun trite popular seasonal congratulations. The commonplace "crane" and "tortoise" echo like empty words, like the actors who come begging on New Year's Eve with empty wishes for prosperity. The customary New Year pine will not stand beside my door. I won't even sweep my dusty house, living as I do in a tiny hermitage constantly threatening to collapse under harsh north winds. I leave it all to the Buddha, as in the ancient story.

The way ahead may be dangerous, steep as snowy trails winding through high mountains. Nevertheless I welcome the New Year just as I am.

New Year greeting-time:
I feel about average
welcoming my spring

Although she was born only last May, I gave my little daughter a bowl of soup and a whole rice cake for New Year's breakfast, saying:

> Laughing, crawling, you're
> exploring—already two[1]
> years old this morning
>
> NEW YEAR'S DAY, 1819

No servant to draw *wakamizu*, New Year's "first water,"

> But look: Deputy
> Crow arrives to enjoy
> the first New Year's bath

Springtime beside a lake:

> Under such a calm
> spring moon, even the tortoise
> crows this season?

As if from the gods,
spring moonlight illuminates
the hillside flower thief

Entering Zenkō Temple on a festival day:

A gray pussy willow
sold as a Buddha flower—
proud among colors

This old cherry tree
was loved famously when it
was—ah—so young

Full cherry blossoms—
his old hip tentative under
tucked-up kimono

Written to celebrate Inari, the mythical trickster fox, on his festival day:

> From among the flowers,
> indifferent to the world,
> foxes bark and cry

> Second day, second month—
> burning moxa with the cat,
> quietly at home[2]

> Emerging brightly,
> beautifully from the bushes,
> a new butterfly!

Ueno Hill in the distance:

> Above the blather,
> those broad walls remain at ease,
> white in misty air

> All the garden this
> poor house can afford: one plot
> of budding green rice

In cherry blossom
shadows, no one, really, is
a stranger now

                V̷

Written on Buddha's Death Day [March 15, 1819]:

Aloof and silent
like the Buddha, I lie still—
still troubled by flowers

Even as he sleeps,
Buddha smilingly accepts
flowers and money

Full of play, the kitten
climbs up on the scale
to weigh itself

Along the Tama River:

Dyers' white cloth strips
luff in the breeze, brightening
the white mists of spring

Two

On a beautiful spring morning, a young monk-in-training named Takamaru, still a child at eleven, left Myōsen Temple with a big monk named Kanryō. They planned to pick herbs and flowers in Araizaka, but the boy slipped on an old bridge and plunged into the icy, roaring river, which was swollen with snowmelt and runoff from Iizuna Mountain.

Hearing the boy's screams for help, Kanryō dashed down the bank, but there was nothing he could do. Takamaru's head bobbed up, then disappeared. A hand rose above the raging water. But soon his cries grew as faint as the high buzz of mosquitoes, and the young monk vanished in the river, nothing left but his image engraved forever on Kanryō's eyes.

On into the evening, torches flared along the bank as people searched for Takamaru. Finally, he was found, his body wedged between boulders, too late for anyone to help.

When someone found a handful of young butterburs in the dead boy's pocket, probably a gift for his parents, even those who seldom weep began to soak their sleeves. They lifted his body onto a bamboo palanquin and carried him home.

It was late evening when his parents ran out to see his

body, their bitter tears observed by everyone. True, as followers of the Way, they had always preached transcendence of this life's miseries, but who could act otherwise? Their all-too-human hearts were shattered by undying love for their child. When the boy had left at dawn, he had been alive and laughing.

The young monk lay still and cold in the evening. Two days later, joining the funeral procession at his cremation, I wrote this tanka:

> Not once did I think
> I'd throw these fresh spring blossoms
> into this dense smoke
> and stand back to watch it rise
> and vanish into the sky.

As much as Takamaru's parents, flowers too must weep to know they may be hacked down and burned on any day just as they open their faces to warm spring sun after months of winter snow. Don't flowers have a life? Won't they, as much as we, realize nirvana in the end?

During meditation:

He glares back at me
with an ugly, surly face,
this old pond frog

A bright moon lights
the plum blossoms. Am I
also tempted to steal them?

High over the dark
shadows of Pine Islands, a
skylark breaks into song

Teasingly, the big cat
wags its long tail, toying with
a small butterfly

Written in Hoshina village on a spring Kannon[3] festival day:

> Wind-strewn blossoms—
> Buddha gathers secret coins
> in a shady nook

> The gentle willow,
> pliant as a woman, tempts me
> into the garden

> Belly full of rice cake,
> to digest, I go out and
> graft another tree

THREE

Several people told me a story about some folks who heard heavenly music at two in the morning on New Year's Day. Furthermore, they all said, these people have heard it again every eighth day since. They described exactly when and where each hearing occurred.

Some people laughed it off as the trickeries of the wind, but I was reluctant to accept or dismiss the story without evidence. Heaven and earth are home to many mysteries. We all know the stories of dancing girls who pour the morning dew from high above. Perhaps the spirits who observe from the corridors of the heavens, seeing a peaceful world, called for music to rejoice. And perhaps we who failed to hear it were deafened by our own suffering.

I invited a few friends to visit my hermitage the morning of March 19th, and we spent the whole night listening. By the time first light broke in the east, we'd heard nothing. Then, suddenly, we heard singing from the plum tree outside a window.

> Just a bush warbler
> to sing morning Lotus Sutra
> to this suffering world

Wanting to welcome
the visiting bush warbler,
I swept the garden

In falling spring rain
the innkeeper assigns rooms,
even to the horse

O little sparrows!
Mind your place! Be careful there!
Lord Horse passes through!

In hazy spring mist,
sitting inside the great hall,
not a hint of sound

Horses pass by, each
with its rider—and behind them,
the skylarks follow

すゞめの子
そこのけ〳〵
お馬が
通る

花光

At Shimabara, Kyoto:

The friendly barker calls—
even the willow's tempted,
bending to a geisha

This rural village
overrun with bamboo shrub—
lucky to see plum

With laughter all day
and nighttime's moons and flowers—
happy new year tides

Countless tea houses
and blossoming cherries all
flower overnight

Hakuhi wrote:

The cherry blossoms
are truly cherry blossoms
only while we wait

I mark passing time
beating straw to weave beneath
this cool summer moon

Composed on Buddha's Birthday anniversary [April
8, 1819]:

Sweet tea and sweet tears
flow wetly over Buddha
through the whole spring day

It must certainly
be a holiday today
even for the rain

After an illness:

I, too, made of dust—
thin and light as the paper
mosquito curtain

With a *splish!* a *splat!*
a few raindrops splash down:
rainy season's done

On the street corner
the blind musician dances,
fan held high overhead

Playing together,
these little baby sparrows
among bamboo shoots

Now the rains have gone,
two neighboring houses
enjoy spring cleaning

On a high, narrow suspension bridge of vine, look-
ing down into a deep valley:

On hands and knees on
a shaky bridge: a cuckoo
cries far below

Summer's first melon
lies firmly hugged to the breast
of a sleeping child

From Ningyō-chō—"Doll Street"—in Edo [Tokyo]:

I thank the doll that serves
my tea, and sit, enjoying
the summer evening breeze

How fortunate! I'm not
punished for dozing behind
the mosquito net

Only just a few
mosquitoes buzzing about—
old people's season!

Hurry now, my flies!
You too may share the riches
of this fine harvest

The small shrine stands
alone, almost lost among
saxifrage blossoms

The quiet life:

    Bending, stretching out,
    the little worm inches along
    my foundation wall

A poem expressing sympathy for a woman recently
widowed and who must now make do for herself:

    Where will you wander
    in your straw hat once this village
    rice is planted?

    Sing hosanna! What
    a beautiful bamboo has
    sprouted overnight!

    Fan tucked politely
    under her collar: hands busy
    picking flowers

    Buzzing noisily
    by my ear, the mosquito
    must know I'm old

年よりと

見てか

鳴く蚊も

耳のそば

花兄

V/

Togakure Mountain poems:

Clear icy water
races straight down the mountain
and into my tub

Whose small hermitage
lies just beyond this spring so
overgrown with moss?

One small mosquito
bites hard, again and again,
attacking in silence

V/

Passing through the gate,
watch your head: you're enjoying
a summer yukata[4]

Lacking a thresher,
I beat the summer wheat
against my house

Poem for a woman peddler in Echigo:

After wheat harvest,
infant on her back, she cries,
"Sardines! Sardines!"

A cut bamboo sprout—
were it not for hungry men
it would have blossomed

A little shady
spot of grass in summertime—
sanctuary

Even this mountain
moss grows flowers all its own—
thus nature bestows

One small mosquito
larva has climbed to where
the new moon shines

Composed at the home of my friend Dokurakubō:

> White saxifrage flowers
> all around my bedroom bring
> me lasting light
>
> In the old temple,
> even the snake has shed
> his worldly skin

Four

I finally decided to visit the far north country, thinking it would be good for my haiku.[5] When I'd filled my pack and shouldered it over my monk's robe, and slipped my beggar's bag around my neck, I was astonished to see. that my shadow looked exactly like the image of the eminent recluse and Zen poet Saigyō [1118–1190]. This observation shamed me when I thought how different his mind from mine: he was fresh, pure, and white as snow, whereas my mind is still dark and windblown as my sleeves.

I departed my old hermitage April 16th, walking stick in hand, but traveled only a few miles when I suddenly realized that I am almost sixty. Like the moon sinking in the western mountains, my life too approaches its final hours.

As I passed through the Shirakawa Barrier, I realized that there was a very good chance I would never again see my home. When a rooster called from a rooftop, I wondered whether he called for me to stop and turn back. A wind over the fields also seemed to beckon me back.

I sat down under a tree to rest my weary legs, and, thinking of the road I'd already traveled, my Kashiwabara village seemed somewhere over the mountains nestled in clouds. Homesick already, I wrote:

> No matter how hard
> I try, I can't stop thinking
> of my old village

The same thoughts written as tanka:

> Memory returns
> to those ancient misty trails
> around my village—
> but neither flowers nor love
> bloom there—only my sadness.

> So very gently
> it won't even disturb
> the butterfly,
> this soft spring wind wanders
> over deep fields of new wheat.

On being idle:

> Mosquito larvae
> are idle—like me today,
> like me tomorrow

Life is brief, desire infinite:

> So many breezes
> wander through my summer room:
> but never enough

> Mornings, the farmer
> studies his green rice fields:
> sown with devotion

I've had this in mind for a long time, trying to find a
way to say it:

> Even the flies
> in the village of my birth
> draw blood with each bite

Here as in heaven
the lotus blooms, growing tall.
But here, much smaller

A summer's estate:
my little grass mat spread out
in the piney shade

Kijō wrote this song for children:

The new dragonfly
circles three times before
it settles in our room

The firefly departs
so quickly, so breathlessly
it leaves its light behind

The old woman
wiped her nose on the blossom
of a moonflower

Calligraphy on
a hot summer day: that boy
wrote on his face

Flitting here and there
a huge firefly dances
across the moor

After enjoying a bath in Nyoi Hot Springs in Tanaka
village:

Lying here looking
at the mountains I just crossed,
I'm even hotter

When I bowed before
the Buddha, hungry mosquitoes
swarmed from his shadow

If you really must
leap, my little fleas, why not
leap on the lotus?

My home is so poor
even the resident flies
keep their family small

That cormorant's my
favorite who surfaces
with an empty beak

A cicada, loud
in the pine—will noontime heat
never arrive?

How fortunate! I'm not
punished for dozing behind
the mosquito net

The free cormorant
scurries back to the boat when
her new baby cries

Five

Everyone kept telling me about remarkably beautiful peonies blooming at the home of my friend Nabuchi. People traveled miles to see them. So I stopped along my way.

Thirty-foot beds were laid under a large canopy, each packed tightly with blossoming white, red, and purple flowers—and more—an especially startling one that was rich black, and another, a strange yellow. Then, as I studied these two more closely, I began to see them as dry and stiff, unlike the vibrant peonies around them. They looked like made-up corpses among beautiful girls.

Of course, Nabuchi made them from paper and tied them to living flowers as a joke for his friends, a truly witty one at that, and without consequence. He asked no fee for viewing his flowers and even provided saké and tea. Laughing about his joke, I wrote:

> Little scraps of paper
> planted among the leaves:
> peony faces

Six

Children hereabouts play a game wherein they bury a live frog and cover its grave with plantain leaves while they sing:

> Hey, hey, the toad is dead,
> the toad is dead.
> Let's all bury it
> under the plantain leaves!
> Under the plantain leaves!

As it happens, an ancient Chinese botanical book, the *Honzō kōmoku*, refers to plantain as "toad's skin," which in this province somehow became "toad's leaf." The game, sprung from the correspondence between Japanese and Chinese common names, must have conveyed some message in earlier times.

> Spindly saxifrage
> bends above the toad's grave
> and its white tears fall

In Chinese mythology, a toad taught a famous hermit how to fly. In Japan, we often credit frogs with having fought bravely at Ten'nōji. But that too is ancient mythology. Today, the toads apparently have made peace with humanity and now live comfortably in the world. If I, for example, should roll out my mat on the ground some summer evening and cry, "Come out, Happy One,[6] come out!"—out of the garden comes a fat toad to sit with me in the cool evening air. That's the soul of a poet! And the greatest honor bestowed upon a toad was when, as written by Chōshōshi, a toad was chosen to judge the Insect Poetry Competition.

> Sitting serenely,
> a plump toad enjoys viewing
> the mountain horizon

Kikaku wrote:

> The oh-so-heavy
> toad crept out to meet the light-
> hearted bush warbler

And Kyokusui wrote:

You've fallen silent,
my toad. Is it all the words
that bloat you so?

Beginning to rain—
the old toad wipes his brow
with the back of his hand

When farmers discuss
rice fields, each thinks his own
is the very best

The mosquito flew
into a woman's bedroom
and died there in flames[7]

Mimicking cormorants,
children dive more cleverly
than real cormorants

Lying in hammocks,
we speak so solemnly of
distant thunder, distant rain

While I was away,
I left the mosquito net
hanging lazily

A flowing freshet—
how the old woodcutter prayed,
deep in the mountains

Searching all this world,
there is no perfect dewdrop
even on the lotus

From high in a tree
the cicada cries after
a wandering puppy

May 28: They say it has rained annually on this day ever since 1193, when the Soga brothers avenged their father's murder at the cost of their own lives. They say the rain commemorates the tears of Tora, wife of one of the brothers.

> Ignoring Tora's
> copious tears, I got soaked,
> drenched to the bone

Seven

In Susaka Township in Shinano Province, a certain Dr. Nakamura, with capricious nastiness, killed a pair of snakes as they were mating. Late that night he was so overcome with searing pain in his penis that it rotted and fell off and he died.

The doctor's son, Santetsu, followed in his father's profession. He was a big man with an enormous mushroom-shaped penis. On his wedding night, however, he was dismayed to find it hanging useless, soft and thin as a candlewick. Overcome with shame, he sought other women, as many as a hundred, hoping to make it with them in order to recover, but always with the same embarrassing result, until he eventually sought refuge in seclusion.

Until I heard this story, I'd never been interested in tales of the supernatural, thinking them no more than regional folktales popularized in old anthologies. But this story prompted me to consider the vengeance of snakes and how the family suffered in turn.

All sentient beings are given life, even fleas and lice, and life is equally dear to each. It is bad enough to kill, but to kill them while they are in the act of procreation is truly terrible.

Imprisoned, the fish
in its tub finds such delight
in fresh cold water

Fly into the mist!
Vanish quickly, my bird! You
are finally free

Ōemaru wrote:

As the mosquito
at equinox sucks my blood,
I sit like Buddha

Mitsutoshi's tanka:

In its final throes,
the dying carp spins, splashing
water with its fins.
Likewise people waste their lives
in useless activities.

Toshiyori wrote:

> Lured by the branches
> set out to trap them, fish thrash
> helplessly about.
> Likewise people are enticed
> by the lures of ignorance.

Written on Mount Asama:

> A lone bindweed root
> holds on for dear life to lava
> on the mountainside

Seeing off a student of haiku:

> Even prickly shrubs
> will do—if you feel a breeze
> pass gently through

Checking stations at mountain passes were established in ancient times to protect travelers, but now they contribute mostly misery:

The gatekeepers burn
moxa for travelers' legs
under blooming plum

Hearing our voices,
the doe moves quickly to stand
beside her fawn

Summer's first firefly,
winging about, ignoring
temptation's sweet call

This slightly bent
lotus stem—appropriate
symbol of our world

The darkness beneath
the canopy of leaves belongs
to listless neighbors

Written beside a large pond:

A single leap—from
waterweed blossom to
that cloud in heaven

I heard about a fellow in a village in Echigo Province who hesitated before offering a night's lodging to the high priest Shinran:

> In Kakikazi,
> even the mountain cuckoo
> stutters nervously

Life in the vast city of Edo:

> A dime-sized patch of grass
> earns just that much of a breeze:
> sweltering weather

> For two *yen* I bought
> enough water to dampen
> my thirsty plant

At Kogane-ga-hara:

> The mare's vigilance:
> watchful while her foal drinks
> deeply from the spring

Those clouds form grandly
high in the sky, but owe it
all to passing winds

Floating together
downriver: the antiplague
sacrament and the flea

At Morin Temple I heard about a badger who meta-
morphosed into a tea kettle:

Here long ago
a tea kettle flew off, light
as a butterfly

When the mosquito
in cherry grove bit me,
I cursed even the blooms

This ant trail must have
begun somewhere in the clouds
in highest heaven

Eight

While visiting the Forest of the Mountain God in Rokugawa village in the Takai area, I picked three small chestnuts, which I eventually planted in the back corner of my garden. One sprouted, lifting up its green head in spring, happy in warm sunlight.

Shortly thereafter, my neighbor on the east remodeled his house, cutting off all the sunlight and moonlight on my chestnut, cutting off even the falling rain and dew. That year it grew little.

All winter, he shoveled the snow from his roof, piling it deep around the building until it looked as if Great White Mountain had been planted there overnight. The narrow pathway on which they carried firewood and water over the summit was steep as the stone steps ascending Atago Mountain. Toward the end of winter, the first happy signs of spring began to appear as green buds spotted the fields, and trees began to blossom. Still the great snowpile remained, deadly white and cold.

Following custom, on April 8th, I prepared to warn away spring woodworms with a poem when a warbler began singing noisily and persistently in the garden. I went out to search for my little chestnut tree buried for months under snow, only to find its broken trunk. Had this tree been human, I'd have sent its remains up in smoke, but it wasn't long before the stump sent out a few small leaves, and by the end of the year it had regained its former height.

Again that winter—and every winter—it was crushed pitilessly by heavy snow. This has happened through seven winters. This unfortunate tree can neither blossom and fruit nor quite die. Its life is a perpetual struggle to survive at a foot in height. Hardly a life for a tree.

And yet my own life closely resembles that of my tree. The firstborn, the first blossom in our family tree, I have been pushed aside to survive among late-blooming weeds, suckled by harsh winds blowing down Stepmother Mountain. I cannot recall a single day when I could freely enjoy life under a wide sky. I don't know how such a thin thread of life could endure fifty-seven long years. Forgive me, my chestnut tree!—I never intended, when I planted you in my garden, for you to share in my own unhappy fate!

One surviving pink,
under shady trees called
Mother Trees, helpless!

Buddha taught that all events have karmic sources. If so, my suffering cannot be without foundation. I must have brought it on myself:

> Even this magnolia,
> merely hanging night and day
> high over my head:
> in springtime it will offer
> many beautiful flowers.

Other poems on this theme include Sōkan's

> All alone, the step-
> child naps on a thin mattress
> of woven grasses

Seishō wrote:

> Sent out to sweep snow
> from bamboo leaves, is that wind
> a stepchild also?

Kōsetsu wrote:

> I'd love to slap that
> fly on the beautiful face
> of my young stepchild

And Mitatsu:

> All night mosquito
> bites multiply the tears
> of the stepchild

In an uncompleted linked verse, Bashō hosted[8] in
1687:

> A well-wrought petition saved
> one from punishment long ago
>
> [TOCHI]

> Thus did a stepmother
> gain a reputation for
> courageous kindness
>
> [RANSETSU]

From another, written by Shoshun and Mitatsu, in the 1691 anthology *Gion Shūi:*

> The servant leaves to bury
> the bodiless head in secret

> The stepmother cries
> through the cold, rainy night
> over her dark crime

From among five linked verses Bashō left in the north country:

> Stained by his doings,
> he stains the blades of grasses
> with bloody business

And Furyū added:

> His stepmother robbed
> him of his rightful life—so
> cut by treachery!

Nine

Once there was a small girl, a stepchild who was not permitted to eat from a clay jar from which her stepsiblings helped themselves to rice balls whenever they fancied. When one day she heard a warbler calling near her window, she wrote a tanka:

> Little bush warbler,
> what makes you cry out so long?
> Do you call for milk,
> enough rice from a clay jar,
> or is your mother gone?

She was the daughter of Lord Tsurayuki.

TEN

I spent my time alone when I was small. I avoided the village children because they teased me. They used to sing:

> Everyone knows the motherless boy;
> he stands alone in the door,
> chewing his thumb from hunger

I sought refuge near the woodpile out back, pitiable, hiding in dark corners, so miserable that, when only six years old, I wrote:

> My little sparrows,
> you too are now motherless—
> come play with me!

ELEVEN

Long ago in Yamato, in Tatsuta village, there lived a particularly cruel woman. Having refused to feed her stepson for ten days, she told him as he was about to die of hunger, "Take this bowl of rice and offer it to the stone roadside Buddha. If he eats, you may also." The boy followed the instructions. But as he sat to pray beside the stone Buddha, it suddenly opened its huge mouth and gobbled the rice almost as if *it* were the starving child.

Thereafter, so the story goes, the woman relaxed her fierce countenance and began to treat her stepson with the same diffidence she extended toward her own children.

Should you ever visit Tatsuta village, you will see that same stone Buddha sitting beside the road, fresh offerings spread before it.

> A stone Buddha in
> a spring breeze by bamboo groves
> enjoys his rice cake

Twelve

Last summer, at bamboo planting time, my wife gave birth to our daughter, whom we named Sato. Born in ignorance, we hoped she would grow in wisdom. On her birthday this year she whirled her arms and head for us and cried. We thought she was asking for a paper windmill, so I bought her one. She tried licking it, then sucking on it, then simply tossed it aside.

Her mind wanders from one thing to the next, never alighting very long on anything. One moment playing with a clay pot, in the next she shatters it. She examines a *shōji* screen, only to rip it open. When we sing her praises, her face lights up. Not a single dark cloud seems to have crossed her mind. She beams like clear moonlight, far more entertaining than the best stage act. When a passerby asks her to point out a dog or bird, she performs with her whole body, head to toe, poised like a butterfly on a grass blade, resting her wings.

She lives in a state of grace. The divine Buddha watches over her. On our annual evening honoring the dead, she comes crawling out as I light the candles on the family altar and ring the prayer bell. She folds her little hands, bending them like bracken shoots, and recites her prayer in a high, sweet voice.

I am old enough for frosty hair, the years add wrinkles to my face. I've not yet found Buddha's grace myself. I've wasted days and nights in empty busyness. It shames me to realize that my daughter, two years old, is closer to Buddhahood than I. But the moment I turn from the altar, I engage in bad karma, despising flies that crawl across my skin, swatting mosquitoes as they buzz about the table, or—worse—drinking wine, which is forbidden by the Buddha.

In the midst of my confession, moonlight falls over the gate like a cool breath. A group of dancing children suddenly begins to sing. My daughter drops her bowl and crawls out on the porch and joins her voice to the others, lifting her hands to the moon. Watching, I forget my advancing age and worldly ways. I daydream about a time when she'll be old enough for long waves of hair, when we encourage her to dance. Surely she could outshine the music of two dozen heavenly maidens. Day in, day out, her legs never rest. By nightfall, she's exhausted and sleeps deeply until the sun is high. While she sleeps, her mother cooks and cleans. Only then can her mother find a moment's rest before she awakens again with a cry. Her mother carries her out to the yard to pee, then nurses her. Our daughter sucks with a smile, poking the breast happily. Her mother then forgets the weariness and pain of having carried her in the womb, she forgets the dirty diapers she washes every day, lost in the supreme joy of having such a child, more precious than jewels.

> Nursing, mother counts
> the fleabites on her daughter's
> small white body

These poems may serve as companion pieces following similar themes:

> A child emerges
> from deep in the willow shade
> with a ghostly face

> Though only a child,
> he bows quietly before
> New Year sacraments

> Asked his age, the boy
> in the bright new kimono
> held up five fingers

Celebratory poem for a small child:

Even faster than
we had dreamed, you have outgrown
your first kimono

Tearfully, the child
begs me to pick the full moon
from the evening sky

In our poor house, the
only family treasures are
children's fireside laughter

Placing the rice cakes
in a row, the child recites,
"Mine!" And "Mine!" And "Mine!"

My daughter struggles
to load her shoulders with
rice cakes for neighbors

The child claps his hands,
playing alone, happily,
under a festive tree

The boy disciplined
by being tied to a tree:
this breeze will cool him down

So ashamed, the child
tied to the tree cries loudly
to passing fireflies

Other poets have written about children.

Teitoku wrote:

Both my baby and
the new year struggled to
their feet this morning

Bashō wrote:

> Without knowing love
> for one's children, there's no truth
> in cherry blossoms

And Shidō:

> Bow to the image!
> Mother's love—helping the child
> slip into his shoes

Rakō wrote:

> Please say it again
> in your sweet little voice, say
> "Flowers!" again!

Tōrai wrote:

> Between window screens,
> a tiny hand reaches out
> to touch the spring rain

And Kisha:

> Her every step
> as she plants rice comes closer
> to her crying child

Kikaku wrote:

> My son has broken
> a blossoming cherry branch.
> How could I punish him?

One hundred days after the birth of my daughter, Kikaku also wrote:

> As I bent to kiss
> my baby's tender cheek,
> I heard the shrike cry

Thirteen

There was a woman, divorced by her husband, who returned to live with her parents while her young son remained with his father. She especially longed to visit her son on Children's Day, but public scorn and humiliation prevented her. She wrote:

> I fly my son's flag
> high, but I venture out only
> as far as the gate

What a true and moving testimonial of a mother's love! If anything can soften the heart of a stony man, it must be a mother's love for her child. Had someone whispered this poem to her husband, he surely would have begged her to return.

Buddha teaches the essential oneness of humanity and nature. If this is true, the love of parent and child must be strongly felt among animals as well, for how could they differ? Onitsura wrote:

The human father
scared away the crow for the
sparrow's children

Gomei wrote:

Warning his children
of danger, father deer calls
from a summer hill

And Tōyō wrote:

A child on his back,
old father frog goes out
to join the chorus

Wind in bamboo leaves
made sounds that brought father deer
bounding for home

From out in dark rain
I heard the plaintive crying
of a fawnless deer

The meadowlark sings,
circling the bushes where
her children hide

FOURTEEN

It is often said that the greatest pleasures result in the greatest misery. But why is it that my little child, who's had no chance to savor even half the world's pleasures—who should be green as new needles on the eternal pine—why should she be found on her deathbed, puffy with blisters raised by the despicable god of smallpox? How can I, her father, stand by and watch her fade away each day like a perfect flower suddenly ravaged by rain and mud?

Two or three days later, her blisters dried to hard scabs and fell off like dirt softened by melting snow. Encouraged, we made a tiny boat of straw and poured hot saké over it with a prayer and sent it floating down-river in hopes of placating the god of the pox. But our hope and efforts were useless and she grew weaker day by day. Finally, at midsummer, as the morning glory flowers were closing, her eyes closed forever.

Her mother clutched her cold body and wailed. I knew her heartbreak but also knew that tears were use-less, that water under the bridge never returns, that scat-tered flowers are gone forever. And yet nothing I could do would cut the bonds of human love.

露の世や

露の世
ながら

さり
ながら

花光

This world of dew
is only the world of dew—
and yet . . . oh and yet . . .

                    ⱱ

As I wrote earlier, I'd left home to travel in the far
north in early spring, but had gotten no farther than
Zenkōji when something made me want to turn back
home again. Hindsight suggests it was the compassion
of Dōso-jin, ancient god of travelers, calling me home.

I made a small anthology of poems treating this and
similar subjects.

Rakugo, on the death of a child:

I search the faces
of dancing children, looking
for one like my child's

Shōhaku wrote this for a small boy who lost his
mother:

On this beautiful
autumn evening he sits
alone at dinner

On the night his daughter was buried, Kikaku wrote:

> The cranes cry in vain
> late into night: no blanket
> can thaw this cold world

Ensui wrote this on the first Girls' Day festival following the death of his granddaughter:

> Going out to store
> away her dolls, I was met
> by huge peach blossoms

Sampū wrote after his daughter died:

> After the full moon,
> I watched it wane, night by night:
> no consolation

Raizan wrote of an adopted boy whose mother had died:

> Nursing the handle
> of his fan, he's still thirsting
> for his late mother

And after the death of his own child:

> I must be crazy
> not to be crazy in this
> crazy spring nightmare

Following the death of his young son, Kaga-no-Chiyo wrote:

> How far has he gone,
> where has he wandered, chasing
> after dragonflies?

V

These poems address the same experience. They were written by ancient noblemen and are given now as I remember them.

An anonymous poem:

> A heartbreaking cry
> from the child sleeping alone
> long after midnight.
> Perhaps in her dreams she longs
> to find her mother beside her.

Tameie wrote:

> Unwanted, the child
> crawls after its mother—
> which brings me to tears.
> For he can neither rise up
> nor face this cold world alone.

Kanesuke wrote:

> A parent's mind may
> not be unenlightened and
> one may nonetheless
> lose one's way completely
> over love for one's child.

In *Mumonkan,* the classic collection of Zen koans, it
is written:

> He comes without lifting a foot;
> he teaches without moving his tongue.
> However you lead the way, remember:
> There is always one you follow.

No sooner received
than it is lost once again,
my little fan

The stag leaps the creek
swollen by spring rains, then looks
back toward his son

I accidentally
learned his name when I found his
fan in the temple

Portrait of a criminal waiting in ambush:

Like a murderer,
the thirsty mosquito hides
in the musky well

On a visit to Ōyama Shrine:

A huge wooden sword—
ten meters long—carried along
by a throng of kimonos!

A comical face—
presenting himself like a clown
with a broad, bright fan

Fifteen

Someone caught a small crow, the size of a lump of coal, and caged it in front of his house in Murasaki village. All night, I listened to the mother flying about, crying in the dark. Moved, I wrote:

> In night's blind darkness,
> fruitlessly searching for
> the baby she loves,
> the mother crow continued
> to cry until sunrise.

Written for the thief caught in his own village:

> In falling spring rain,
> a bird circles fresh bait:
> in his own village

A sympathetic poem for innocent birds eating food put out in the shogun's hunting grounds:

> Two cranes, side by side,
> forage on, unwittingly.
> One will soon be dead

Risshi wrote:

> As the doe nurses
> her newborn fawn, the arrow
> has eyes to find her

Even the most heartless hunter must be humbled by such cruelty and renounce the ways of this world.

Sixteen

My village lies so high on Kurohime Mountain that by the time last winter's snows have melted in the summer sun, autumn frost has already begun. Trees imported from warmer regions undergo changes, as with a mandarin orange, grown to but half its normal size—like one I read about in a Chinese book.

> The primrose should grow
> nine distinct blossoms—but here,
> only four or five

On the ancient battleground where, as the legend goes, Chinzei Hachirō Tametomo threw down his enemies like stones, I borrowed his words to write:

> Listen, enemies
> low as worms, hear the piercing
> cry of the cuckoo!

On the deer's tongue, the
cluster of flowering clover
rests so easily!

I remember a famous painting of an ancient Chinese
sage standing on a rock, handing a scroll to a young
man:

"I've waited for you
for a long time"—for your song,
my mountain cuckoo

The quiet life:

My home is quiet.
The cuckoo's song is silenced
in my quiet home

Eluding the hands
of a man, the firefly
quickly disappears

"You can't fool me!" cries
the little firefly as it
flits quickly away

Seventeen

Ōritsu wrote recently to tell me that Seikeishi is gone, his voice silenced last winter.

> What you do or don't
> say really doesn't matter:
> talking to dead trees

> A wanderer rests
> in green shade, giving his hat
> a chance to breathe

> "The honorable
> Lord Toad, Marshland Overseer,
> happy to meet you!"

> That fat toad looks like
> he just burped a huge cloud
> filling the sky

Withering red leaves
fall so festively in
cool green summer shade

With each lightning flash,
each roll of thunder, rice and
the world grow richer

Seen in a flash
of lightning, the riverbed
looks utterly dead

Even on foggy
nights, the horse can avoid
the hole in the bridge

Helpless against this
autumn wind, the firefly
must crawl from my hand

Written one afternoon during a rest in a field:

Protecting the child
from the cold autumn wind,
the old scarecrow

On losing my traveling companion:

> At sunset this fall
> evening, I wrote on a wall:
> "I've gone on ahead"

Midsummer, visiting my daughter's grave seventeen days after her death:

> In soft pampas grass
> I sit a long time before
> saying my prayer

> When the evening drum
> begins, even the woodpecker
> stops to listen

> So studiously!
> the old woodpecker assays
> my hermitage

In a temple storehouse:

> Smiling serenely,
> the Buddha gently points to
> a little stinkworm

Like an acrobat
balanced very proudly on
one leg: the wild goose

A mountain temple—
hearing the stag's piercing cry
from the balcony

The high distant cry
of the stag tells the hunter
how to blow his horn

Chattering, they return
from the mountains empty-handed,
the mushroom pickers

Visiting my daughter's grave on July 25th, one
month after her death:

The red flower
you always wanted to pick—
now this autumn wind

A few blossoms fall
from the deer's munching mouth:
flowering clover

How well we have slept
to feel so fresh this morning,
dear chrysanthemums!

What a perfect night
for doing almost nothing—
cool enough for a stroll

Trying to pick up
the dewdrop, the child's amazed—
it disappears!

Eighteen

"Find shelter beneath the biggest tree," as the saying goes. There are always those who are all too eager to bow to the rich, who oil their tongues whenever they are in the presence of those who wield power.

Near Suwa Shrine in this village, a huge old chestnut grows. Although it doesn't seem unusually heavy with nuts, no one who passes every morning can resist picking up at least a few chestnuts.

Nineteen

From Nashimoto's house in Takaino, I watched the full
moon rise:

> All alone at home,
> my wife, like me, is watching
> this full moon rise

I watched an eclipse of the moon beginning at ten,
reaching total eclipse at midnight, and continuing until
two in the morning.

> The nature of man:
> the moon gazers vanish
> more quickly than the moon

> In this temporal world,
> even this bright full moon must
> endure its eclipse

> Pretending wisdom,
> a man tells a woman all
> about the eclipse

After emptying
our cups, we sat down to view
the late night moon

𝖵

No one recognizes the smell of his own bean paste:

Village peasants sing
praises for this "Soba Country"
under a full moon

𝖵

In September I attended a chrysanthemum-viewing
party at the home of my friend Shōfūin:

Like an aging harvest
god, my hoe rests on his
among chrysanthemums

With wine cups in hand
we wander in a garden
of chrysanthemums

With a stick in hand
like a priest, our host lectures
on chrysanthemums

A towel for a headband,
a bald head labors slowly
among chrysanthemums

How beautiful! these
chrysanthemums—but sadly
our host does not drink

In a dream I saw my daughter's smiling face:

My daughter brushes
her smooth cheek with a melon
only in my dream

Driven from the fields
by men, wandering birds
pass through the village

Among hoop-shaped twigs
and leaves, titmice show off
performing tricks

His patience expired,
from high in his treetop
the old shrike cries

With body and soul
this skinny little mantis
met every struggle

Written on the mountainside above Takaino village:

In the autumn wind
I study those old mountains
using my compass

Lit by a lamp hung
in a pine, village women
are washing their clothes

You remain with me,
old wild goose, no matter where
you roam—same autumn night

Advice written on the fan of a young priest:

There's your long shadow!
For shame! Wandering around
on a cold dark night

Hakuhi wrote:

Passing high above
our village, migrating birds cry,
"Nobody needs you!"

And Shiei wrote:

The old wine seller
offers a brand-new saké
from his green shade

I dreamt of finding myself in peaceful old age:

> Secretly saying
> heartfelt thanks to my children
> this cool autumn night

> No more than shadow,
> a cricket in the yellow dust
> of the harvester

> Little chrysanthemum,
> unlike the snared thief, you
> needn't feel ashamed

Lost in the dark:

> "The sewage ditch
> is over here!" the old horse
> calls in midnight cold

> No quarreling
> on your migration, dear birds—
> help find the way

Standing side by side,
two bucks lick ice and frost
from each other's skin

"Wolf scat!" Just the words
are enough to send icy
shivers down my spine

Used for scrubbing wine
barrels, these fresh maple leaves
were plucked in their prime

With just the slightest
parting of my lips, thousands
of plovers take flight

A good day begins
with charcoal popping hot
and a good deep cough

An autumn drizzle—
faintly, the wooden Buddha-drum—
bathhouse workers come

Blown by gusts of wind,
the blind masseur blows his whistle
unsuccessfully

∿

Watching a beggar on the walkway at Zenkō
Temple:

The beggar remains
sitting in evening rain—
few coins in his box

∿

Backwards, ass over
teakettle, the small boy held
fast to his radish

The first snow has fallen
and now lies alone and white
out behind our house

A servant scurries
across Bridge of Frost into
the teeth of the wind

After the sermon,
a gracious farmer invites me
to stroll in his field

Just a few snowflakes
from the sky above Shinano:
I don't know one joke

Suspicious character
maybe, but no crook, though I'm
confined by winter

On hearing about burglars roaming around the
village:

Frosty autumn nights
my house is overrun
by noisy watchmen

What's said of snowmen
doesn't last any longer
than the snowmen

Mother proudly
demonstrates how to make good
rice cake offerings

Happy, the children
tell of hearing rice cake pounding
at our neighbor's house

On approaching New Year:

Don't complain: rice cake
flowers will soon blossom
on our willow tree

When year-end beggars
dance down our street, elders sing
louder than children

Along the road to Edo:

An easy target:
on the main road, they call me
"another starling"[9]

In Gojiingahara:

> The old prostitute's
> tawdry hovel shudders in
> piercing winter wind

At Ryōgoku Bridge:

> Time to purify:
> midwinter water dragons
> writhe across men's backs[10]

Someone told me about a man who, retiring to the far side of the Kamo River, vowed never to cross it again. Lacking his strength of conviction, I left my mountain village sanctuary, white hair blown by the wind, to return again to the famous city:

> Another year older,
> ashamed to be returning
> to Edo again

> "Good luck begin!
> Throw out all the demons!"[11]
> —voices of children

Left to their own devices, people often choose harmful ways:

> In my hermitage
> winter poverty drives me
> to eat many strange things[12]

> ✓

Winter solstice, the beginning of spring:

> On this holiday
> they say, a single cry
> drives demons away

> From today forward,
> each green new stalk of wheat adds
> to our New Year riches

At the year's end, it is the Shinto custom to hang New Year prayer cards and wishes all around the shrine:

> The blossoming plum
> stoop-shouldered like an old man
> loaded with wishes

Twenty

A week after solstice, a beautiful day:
My wife rose early to make a fine breakfast. On this day in years past, our neighbor Sonoemon had always made rice cakes and generously sent us some. So it was natural that we anticipated having his fresh, warm rice cakes with our breakfast. We waited. We waited longer. Nothing arrived. Eventually, we turned to our breakfast, which had long since grown cold.

> Only a memory:
> our neighbor's tasty rice cakes
> at our gate as before

Twenty-one

People who believe that only faith can bring salvation and who think on nothing else are snared ever more tightly by the web of their own willfulness. Their hell is their own clinging to the idea of salvation. Likewise, there are some who remain inactive, believing they are enlightened; believing that Buddha, more than they themselves, can rectify their hearts. They too fail to understand. So where is a solution? The answer is simple: we should put aside the issue of salvation; neither great faith nor personal virtue is enough. We must place our trust in the way of Buddha. Whether we find ourselves in heaven or in hell, he reveals the innermost secret. Only in following his way can we surrender our self-obsessions—busy spiders weaving our webs of desire across the world, greedy farmers stealing our neighbors' water. When our minds are at peace, there's no need for constantly reciting prayers with an empty voice. We follow the way of Buddha. Salvation is the peace of mind found in the teaching. Blessings in the name of Buddha:

> Beyond good or bad,
> with Buddha, I say good-bye
> to the passing year

WRITTEN DECEMBER 29, 1819, AT AGE FIFTY-SEVEN

SELECTED HAIKU

So much money made
by clever temple priests
using peonies

Kane moke
jozu na tera no
botan kana

New Year greeting-time:
I feel about average,
welcoming my spring

Medetasa mo
chūgurai nari
ora ga haru

Simply for all this,
as if there were nothing else,
heavy wet spring frost

Korekiri to
miete dossari
haru no shimo

Even my shadow
enjoys good health and is safe
on spring's first bright day

Kageboshi mo
mame sokusai de
kesa no haru

Even the turtle
can tell the time by watching
this bright spring moon

Suppon mo
toki ya tsukuran
haru no tsuki

It is New Year's Day,
but nothing's changed at my
unkempt hermitage

Ganjitsu mo
betsujō no naki
kuzu-ya kana

Once snows have melted,
the village soon overflows
with friendly children

Yuki tokete
mura ippai no
kodomo kana

The small butterfly
moves as though unburdened by
the world of desire

·Chō tobu ya
kono yo ni nozomi
nai yō ni

A bird is singing
somewhere within the grove, but
no plum blossoms yet

Tori no ne ni
sakō to mo sezu
ume no hana

あっさりと若葉来にけり
あさぎ空

花兄

By the entranceway,
waving invitingly,
a willow grows

Iriguchi no
aiso ni nabiku
yanagi kana

It is not very
eager to blossom, this
plum tree by the gate

Hitasura ni
sakō de mo nashi
kado no ume

Today and today
also—a kite entangled
in a gnarled tree

Kyō mo kyō mo
tako hikkakaru
enoki kana

As simple as that—
spring has finally arrived
with a pale blue sky

Assari to
haru wa ki ni keri
asagi-zora

At the very edge
of the contaminated well
a plum tree blossoms

Kusa-mizu no
ido no kiwa yori
ume no hana

The young sparrows
return into Jizō's sleeve[13]
for sanctuary

Suzume no ko
jizō no sode ni
kakurekeri

"Let's visit bamboo!
Let's go visit the plum tree!"
mother sparrow cries

Take ni iza
ume ni iza to ya
oya-suzume

All around my house,
pond frogs, from the beginning,
sang about old age

Waga io ya
kawazu shote kara
oi wo naku

Entering the gate,
he is simply oblivious,
the wandering frog

Waga kado e
shiranande hairu
kawazu kana

A child has drawn
a river from snowmelt lakes
leading to my gate

Monzen ya
tsue de tsukurishi
yukige-gawa

A gust of spring wind—
unhappily—lifts the skirts
of the roof thatcher

Harukaze ni
shiri wo fukaruru
yaneya kana

In falling spring mist
the cat learns festival dance—
taught by a small girl

Harusame ya
neko ni odori wo
oshieru ko

As old age arrives,
considering just the day's length
can move one to tears

Oinomi wa
hi no nagai ni mo
namida kana

Like the poet Saigyō,
he sits there singing his song,
this skinny old frog!

Saigyō no
yō ni suwatte
naku kawazu

He glares back at me
with an ugly, surly face,
this old pond frog

Ware wo mite
nigai kao suru
kawazu kana

He's the overseer
croaking orders from his throne,
Big Boss Frog!

*Oyabun to
miete jōza ni
naku kawazu*

With such a voice
you should also learn to dance,
bellowing frog

*Sono koe de
hitotsu odore yo
naku kawazu*

Among tea flowers,
the little sparrows play
hide-and-seek

*Cha no hana ni
kakurenbo suru
suzume kana*

If you are kindly,
they will shit all over you,
happy young sparrows

Jihi sureba
hako wo suru nari
suzume no ko

In the middle of
a horde of noisy children—
one tired sparrow

Ōzei no
ko ni tsukaretaru
suzume kana

At Zenkō Temple,
as if tired from their pilgrimage,
small sparrows look back

Zenkōji e
itte kita kao ya
suzume no ko

Lonely Ojizō!¹⁴
Smiling serenely among
pink flower blossoms

Ojizō ya
hana nadeshiko no
mannaka ni

The sleeping puppy
continues gnawing on
the willow tree

Inu no ko no
kuwaete nemuru
yanagi kana

The little puppy
doesn't know autumn's arrived.
But he's still a Buddha!

Aki kinu to
shiranu enoko ga
hotoke kana

In falling spring rain—
such an enormous yawn from
a beautiful woman

Harusame ni
ōakubi suru
bijin kana

He sits all alone
in freezing rain for us all,
this great stone Buddha

Hito no tame
shigurete owasu
hotoke kana

All of us foolish
on this moonlit night after
ten nights of sutras

moromoro no
gusha mo tsukiyo no
jūya kana

So small! Perilously
clinging to Mount Fuji,
the young willow

Chonbori to
fuji no kowaki no
yanagi hana

Envious even
of the child being punished
on New Year's Eve

Shikararuru
hito urayamashi
toshi no kure

A butterfly
flutters past—my body feels
the dust of ages

Chō tonde
waga mi mo chiri no
tagui kana

In their bamboo hats
they whisper "Good-bye, good-bye,"
in a falling mist

Kasa de suru
saraba saraba ya
usugasumi

It's regrettable
that you follow after me,
little butterfly

Kinodoku ya
ore wo shitōte
kuru kochō

At the flowerpot,
the butterfly listens:
true Buddha Dharma

Hanaoke ni
chō mo kiku kayo
ichidaiji

In a warm spring rain
a rat is slowly drinking
Sumida River

Harusame ya
nezumi no nameru
sumidagawa

Dear evening swallow,
today is a burden—and
trust nothing tomorrow!

Yūtsubame
ware ni wa asu no
ate mo nashi

A new fawn twitches,
shaking free a butterfly,
then naps once again

Saoshika ya
chō wo furutte
mata nemuru

The morning glories,
blossoming, have thatched the roof
of my hermitage

Asagao no
hana de fukitaru
iori kana

In a light spring rain
a discarded letter blows
through a bamboo grove

Harusame ya
yabu ni fukaruru
sute-tegami

The winter wren
goes about her business
without a sound

Kossori to
shite kasegu nari
misosazai

The field wren,
searching here, there, everywhere—
has she lost something?

Misosazai
kyoro kyoro nan zo
otoshita ka

Graciously, the dog
steps out of my way along
this snowy trail

Inudomo ga
yokete kurekeri
yuki no michi

I know everything
about the old householder,
even his shiver

Mi ni sou ya
mae no aruji no
samusa made

By a neighbor's light
I sit in a rented room:
cold and cold food tonight!

Tsugi no ma no
hi de zen ni tsuku
samusa kana

Stopping at the gate,
I hear the Mii Temple bell,
sound frozen in the air

Kadoguchi ni
kite kōru nari
mii no kane

Good company,
the cat sits among us
on New Year's Eve

Onakama ni
neko mo za toru ya
toshiwasure

The third crescent moon,
this spring night so very cold
its back too is curved

Mikazuki wa
soru zo samusa wa
saekaeru

Freezing moonlight falls
on the legs of great Nio guards
at the temple gate

Kangetsu ni
tatsu ya niō no
karassune

Fast as it can go—
sailing into the fire—
a single hailstone![15]

Abaraya ni
tonde hi ni iru
arare kana

The hail has fallen—
in moonlight the young hookers
quietly return

Tama arare
yotaka wa tsuki ni
kaerumeri

Like the burning
of this charcoal fire, our years
too will soon expire

Sumi no hi ya
yowai no heru mo
ano tōri

Only a few people
at a glance; at a glance, leaves
fall here, leaves fall there

Hito chirari
konoha mo chirari
horari kana

Buddha beside a field,
and blooming from his nose,
a long icicle

Nobotoke no
hana no saki yori
tsurara kana

My father also
studied these high mountains
from his winter hut

Oya mo kō
mirareshi yama ya
fuyugomori

The young bush warbler,
with a bright yellow voice,
calls for its parents

Uguisu ya
kiiro na koe de
oya wo yobu

Even in good light
the guy in this self-portrait
looks awfully cold

Hiikime ni
mite sae samuki
soburi kana

"The sewage ditch
is over here!" the old horse
calls in midnight cold

Shōbenjo
koko to uma yobu
yosamu kana

Early this morning,
falling silently, a single
paulownia leaf

Kesa hodo ya
kosori to ochite
aru hitoha

The turnip farmer
with a turnip points the way
back to the road

Daikohiki
daiko de michi wo
oshiekeri

Trembling helplessly
like a solitary heart,
this pampas grass stalk

Hosusuki ya
hosoki kokoro no
sawagashiki

I am leaving now.
You may play together
happily, crickets!

Dete iku zo
naka yoku asobe
kirigirisu

Be a good friend and
tend to our house while I'm gone,
my little cricket!

*Otonashiku
rusu wo shite iro
kirigirisu*

Take care in the grass—
don't wipe out those pearls of dew,
little cricket!

*Shiratsuyu no
tama fungaku na
kirigirisu*

Tell me as you go,
wild goose, how often you've seen
Mount Asama's smoke

*Kaeru kari
asama no keburi
ikudo miru*

Keeping the infant
safe from harsh autumn wind:
the old scarecrow

Chinomigo no
kazeyoke ni tatsu
kagashi kana

Beautiful full moon—
nothing extraordinary
to the old scarecrow

Meigetsu ni
kerorito tachishi
kagashi kana

Where does it come from,
such bitter winter cold,
I ask you, scarecrow?

Dochira kara
samuku naru zo yo
kagashi-dono

The moor crow is so
satisfied, having landed
on the *bashō* tree

Nogarasu no
jōzu ni tomaru
bashō kana

Calm, indifferent
as if nothing's transpired—
the goose, the willow

Kerorikan
to shite kari to
yanagi kana

"A party of one,"
the innkeeper duly noted.
A cold autumn night

Ichinin to
chōmen ni tsuku
yosamu kana

People! Compelled to go
when not even a scarecrow
remains standing

Hito wa isa
suguna kagashi mo
nakarikeri

Just beyond my reach,
that chestnut is inviting:
what color! what size!

Hirowarenu
kuri no migoto yo
ōkisa yo

Rice piled everywhere,
Jizō looks even more lonely
by this country road

Ine tsunde
jizō wabishi ya
michi no hata

The sacred night dance:
as bonfires pop and cackle,
painted leaves fall in

Yokagura ya
takibi no naka e
chiru momiji

When I finally die,
I hope you'll tend my grave,
little grasshopper!

Ware shinaba
hakamori to nare
kirigirisu

Snowy white dew—and
above the potato fields,
the River of Heaven

Shiratsuyu ya
imo no hatake no
amanogawa

Thus spring begins: old
stupidities repeated,
new errors invented

Haru tatsu ya
gu no ue ni mata
gu ni kaeru

Just beyond the gate,
a neat yellow hole—
someone pissed in the snow

Massugu na
shōben-ana ya
kado no yuki

With this rising bath-mist
deep in a moonlit night,
spring finally begins

Yukeburi mo
tsukiyo no haru to
nari ni keri

People working rice fields,
from my deepest heart, I bow.
Now a little nap

Ta no hito wo
kokoro de ogamu
hirune kana

In the beggar's tin
a few thin copper coins
and this evening rain

Jubako no
zeni shigomon ya
yūshigure

For you too, my fleas,
the night passes so slowly.
You too are lonely

Nomidomo mo
yonaga daro zo
sabishi karo

Brilliant moon,
is it true that you too
must be busy?

Meigetsu ya
kyo wa anata mo
isogashiki

The winter fly
I caught and finally freed
the cat quickly ate

Fuyu no hae
nigaseba neko ni
torarekeri

A faint yellow rose
almost hidden in deep grass—
and then it moves

Yamabuki ya
kusa ni kakurete
mata soyogu

Mother, I weep
for you as I watch the sea
each time I watch the sea

Naki-haha ya
umi miru tabi ni
miru tabi ni

As the great old trees
are marked for felling, the birds
build their new spring nests

Kiru ki tomo
shirade ya tori no
su wo tsukuru

Like misty moonlight,
watery, bewildering—
our temporal way

Oboro oboro
fumeba mizu nari
mayoi michi

My dear old village,
every memory of home
pierces like a thorn

Furusato ya
yoru mo sawaru mo
bara no hana

A sheet of rain.
I remain alone among
cherry blossom shadows

Furu ame ni
hitori nokori shi
hana no kage

A flowering plum
and a nightingale's love song—
yet I am alone

Ume sakedo
uguisu nakedo
hitori kana

My old village lies
far beyond what we can see,
but there the lark sings

*Furusato no
mienaku narite
naku hibari*

This world of dew
is only a world of dew—
and yet . . . oh and yet . . .

*Tsuyu no yo wa
tsuyu no yo nagara
sarinagara*

This suffering world:
the flowers will blossom, but
even at that . . .

*Ku no shaba ya
sakura ga sakeba
saita tote*

Swatting the housefly
on the blossom, I also crush
the flower

Hae uchi ni
hana saku kusa mo
utare keri

Here in Shinano
are famous moons, and buddhas,
and our good noodles

Shinano de wa
tsuki to hotoke to
ora ga soba

When the wild turnip
burst into full blossom
a skylark sang

No daiko mo
hana saki ni keri
naku hibari

The distant mountains
are reflected in the eye
of the dragonfly

Tōyama ga
medama ni utsuru
tombo kana

What's the lord's vast wealth
to me, his millions and more?
Dew on trembling grass

Nan no sono
hyakumangoku mo
sasa no tsuyu

Before this autumn wind
even the shadows of mountains
shudder and tremble

Akikaze ya
hyoro hyoro yama no
kageboshi

This year on, forever,
it's all gravy for me now—
spring playtime arrives

Kotoshi kara
marumoke zo yo
shaba asobi

I wish she were here
to listen to my bitching
and enjoy this moon

Kogoto iu
aite mo araba
kyo no tsuki

Gratitude for gifts,
even snow on my bedspread
a gift from the Pure Land

Arigata ya
fusuma no yuki mo
Jodo yori

The old dog listens
intently, as if to the
work songs of the worms

Furu inu ya
mimizu no uta ni
kanji-gao

As it grows colder
every night, even the songs
of worms grow fainter

Usosamu ya
mimizu no uta mo
hitoyo zutsu

My spring is just this:
a single bamboo shoot,
a willow branch

Waga haru wa
take ippon ni
yanagi kana

やれうつな

はえが

手を

する

足を

する

花兒

From that woman
on the beach, dusk pours out
across ebbing tides

Onna kara saki e
kasumu zo
shiohigata

Don't kill that poor fly!
He cowers, wringing
his hands for mercy

Yare utsu na
hae ga te wo suri
ashi wo suru

Before I arrived,
who were the people living here?
Only violets remain

Waga mae ni
dare dare sumi shi
sumire zo mo

At this lonely grave,
the one constant visitor
is a winter wren

Ara sabishi
tsuka wa itsumo no
misosazai

Nearly frostbitten,
the village prostitute scrapes
soot from an iron pan

Shimogare ya
nabe no sumi kaku
kokeisei

The maidenflower,
amazingly, stands idly
in the empty field

Ominaeshi
akkerakon to
tateri keri

A mountain temple—
hearing the stag's piercing cry
from the balcony

Yamadera ya
en no ue naru
shika no koe

O autumn winds,
tell me where I'm bound, to which
particular hell

Aki no kaze
.ware wa mairu wa
dono jigoku

From the Great Buddha's
great nose, a swallow comes
gliding out

Daibutsu no
hana kara detaru
tsubame kana

A world of dew,
and within every dewdrop
a world of struggle

*Tsuyu no yo no
tsuyu no naka nite
kenka kana*

Naturally,
I bow my head on holy
Kamiji Mountain

*Onozukara
zu ga sagaru nari
kamijiyama*

Peeking through the fence
on a tranquil sunny day—
a young mountain monk

*Nodokasa ya
kakima wo nozoku
yama no sō*

Under this bright moon
I sit like an old buddha
knees spread wide

Meigetsu ya
hotoke no yo ni
hiza wo kumi

.

My noontime nap
sweetened by voices singing
rice-planting songs

Motaina ya
hirune shite kiku
taue-uta

Today and today
and today the bamboo's watched
by the brazier

Kyō mo kyō mo
kyō mo take miru
hioke kana

.

In the midst of this world
we stroll along the roof of hell
gawking at flowers

Yo no naka wa
jigoku no ue no
hanami kana

Give me a homeland,
and a passionate woman,
and winter alone

Kimi ga yo wa
onna mo sunari
fuyu gomori

While the street-corner
priest continues to blather—
ah!—tranquillity

Tsuji dangi
chinpunkan mo
nodoka kana

A world of trials,
and if the cherry blossoms,
it simply blossoms

Ku no shaba ya
sakura ga sakeba
saita tote

In my hidden house,
no teeth left in the mouth,
but good luck abounds

Kakurega ya
ha no nai kuchi de
fuku wa uchi

So many fleabites,
but on her lovely young skin
they are beautiful

Nomi no ato
sore mo wakaki wa
utsukushiki

Now we are leaving,
the houseflies can make love
to their heart's desire

Rusu ni suru zo
koi shite asobe
io no hae

The blossoming plum!
Today all the fires of hell
remain empty

Ume saku ya
jigoku no kama mo
kyujitsu to

Just to say the word
home, that one word alone,
so pleasantly cool

Waga yado to
iu bakari de mo
suzushisa yo

This year's hottest day:
some nasty fellow stole
my umbrella!

*Futatsu naki
kasa nusumareshi
doyo kana*

How comfortable
my summer cotton robe
when drenched with sweat

*Omoshiro ya
ase no shimitaru
yukata kana*

Chrysanthemum blooms—
even the stench of urine
succumbs to its perfume

*Shōben no
ka mo kayoi keri
kiku no hana*

On this spindly plant,
finally, one shabby
blossom has arrived

Yasekusa no
yoro yoro hana to
nari ni keri

In this mountain village,
shining in my soup bowl,
the bright moon arrives

Yamazato wa
shiru no naka made
meigetsu zo

After a long nap,
the cat yawns, rises, and goes out
looking for love

Nete okite
ōakubi shite
neko no koi

O summer snail,
you climb but slowly, slowly
to Fuji's summit

Katatsumuri
soro soro nobore
fuji no yama

It is true even
among this world's insects:
some sing well, some not

Yo no naka ya
naku mushi ni sae
jōzu heta

Weakened by illness,
breaking this blossoming branch,
my mouth turns down

Otoroe ya
hana wo oru ni mo
kuchi mageru

Lying, arms and legs
splayed out, how supremely cool,
how sweetly lonely

Dai no ji ni
nete suzushisa yo
sabishisa yo

Sweaty summer night:
spent almost sleeping between
mounds of baggage

Atsuki yo no
ni to ni no aida ni
netarikeri

Pouncing, the kitten
tackles and holds down the leaf—
for the moment

Neko no ko no
choi to osaeru
konoha kana

The mountain warbler
lives by virtue of these
falling autumn leaves

Uguisu no
kuchisugi ni kuru
ochiba kana

Evening clouds disperse:
under a pale sky, a range
of autumn mountains

Yūbare ya
asagi ni narabu
aki no yama

That old woodpecker
keeps working his tree even
as day turns to evening

Kitsutsuki ya
hitotsu tokoro ni
hi no kururu

Another useless man,
I walk the night alone
beneath a cold moon

Muda hito ya
fuyu no tsukiyo wo
bura bura to

The mountain water
is busy pounding the rice
while I enjoy a nap

Yama mizu ni
kome wo tsukasete
hirune kana

O moonlit blossoms—
I've squandered forty-nine years
walking beneath you

Tsuki hana ya
shijuku-nen no
muda aruki

Spring has come again,
and it couldn't be better,
oh, blossoming plum!

Waga haru mo
jōjō kichi yo
ume no hana

Ask tearfully, truly—
even the flowers are falling,
falling to the ground

Tada tanome
.hana mo hara hara
ano tōri

From this day forward,
you will be Japanese geese—
may you thrive in peace

Kyō kara wa
nihon no kari zo
raku ni neyo

Bright autumn moonlight:
countless sea lice come rushing
over the stones

Meigetsu ya
funamushi hashiru
ishi no ue

I live as I do
and no matter—the tortoise
lives ten thousand years

Ā mama yo
ikite mo kame no
hyaku-bu ichi

The huge firefly,
a little wobbly on its wings,
comes fluttering by

Ō botaru
yurari yurari to
tōri keri

大鹽
ゆるりくと
通りけり

花光

With my folding fan
I measured the peony—
as it demanded

Ōgi nite
shaku wo toraseru
botan kana

Futility
in the gaping mouth of
the sparrow's stepchild

Mata muda ni
kuchi aku tori no
mamako kana

A fruitful year—
flies gather on the grass,
singing happily

Hōnen no
koe wo agekeri
kusa no hae

At the Zen temple,
pine needles silently fall
through the godless month

Zendera ni
matsu no ochiba ya
kannazuki

Autumn evening—
the hole in my *shōji* sounds like
a flute being blown

Aki no yo ya
shōji no ana no
fue wo fuku

My tired legs spread
comfortably—overhead,
a few passing clouds

Nagedashita
ashi no saki nari
kumo no mine

In a bitter wind
they wait—two bits per trick—
outside a whore's shack

Kogarashi ya
nijū-yon-mon no
yūjo goya

Winter hermitage:
from the first night, listening
to rain on the mountain

Fuyugomori
sono yo ni kiku ya
yama no ame

Blown softly away
in rustling breezes, spring leaves
fields of new grasses

Yusa-yusa to
haru ga yuku zo yo
nobe no kusa

For our rice country,
only most superior
scorching summer heat!

Kome-guni no
jōjō-kichi no
atsusa kana

On the hottest day,
single-mindedly, a crow
buries its secret

Atsuki hi ni
naniyara umeru
karasu kana

Be calm, skinny frog!
Now that Issa's on his way,
you needn't worry

Yasegaeru
makeru na issa
kore ni ari

This mountain moonlight
gently illuminates
the flower thief

Yama no tsuki
hana nusubito wo
terashi tamō

All around my house,
pond frogs, from the beginning,
sang about old age

Waga io ya
kawazu shote kara
oi wo naku

How joyous and kind!
In my next life, let me be
a butterfly afield

Mutsumashi ya
umare-kawaraba
nobe no chō

Fly, butterfly!
I feel the dust of this world
weighting my body!

Chō tonde
waga mi mo chiri no
tagui kana

Under shady trees
resting with a butterfly—
this, too, is karma

Ki no kage ya
chō to yasumu mo
tashō no en

The field worker
wipes his snotty fingers
on the plum blossom

Hatauchi ya
tebana wo nejiru
ume no hana

The great *daimyō*
slowly dismounts from his horse—
cherry blossoms

Daimyō wo
uma kara orosu
sakura kana

Just being alive!
—miraculous to be in
cherry blossom shadows!

Kō ikite
iru mo fushigi zo
hana no kage

Pain and suffering—
even if the old cherry
had somehow blossomed

Ku no shaba ya
sakura ga sakeba
saita tote

Evening cherry
blossoms—now this day too
enters history

Yū-zakura
kyō mo mukashi ni
nari ni keri

"Cherry blossoms, cherry blossoms!"
the old folk song went,
praising this old tree

Sakura sakura to
utawareshi
oiki kana

Among blooming flowers
we continue our writhing—
all living beings

Saku hana no
naka ni ugomeku
shujō kana

Where Kannon remains—
every endless direction—
the cherries blossom

*Kannon no
aran kagiri wa
sakura kana*

Truly heaven-sent,
drifting down from everywhere,
these cherry blossoms

*Ten kara de mo
futtaru yō ni
sakura kana*

After evening bath
and bows before the Buddha—
these cherry blossoms

*Yu mo abite
hotoke ogande
sakura kana*

People whispering—
listening, they blush a bit,
evening cherry blossoms

Hitogoe ni
hotto shita yara
yūzakura

It was my favorite
place for cherry blossom shade,
now gone forever

Kiniitta
sakura no kage mo
nakari keri

Stone River's rushing
waters lit by bright flashes
of lightning

Ishikawa wa
guwarari inazuma
sarari kana

Loneliness already
planted with each seed in
morning glory beds

Haya sabishi
asagao maku to
yū hatake

.

Today, today too,
somehow getting by these days, still
living in a haze

Kyō mo kyō mo
kasunde kurasu
koie kana

In early spring rain
the ducks that were not eaten
are quacking happily

Harusame ya
kuware-nokori no
kamo ga naku

.

From birthing's washbowl
to the washbowl of the dead—
blathering nonsense!

Tarai kara
tarai ni utsuru
chinpunkan

Notes

1. Traditionally in many Asian cultures, babies are considered to be one year old when they are born.
2. Moxa was burned and rubbed on the legs before travel and also burned on the trip as an incense to ward off Inari.
3. Kannon (Kuan Yin in Chinese) is the bodhisattva of compassion.
4. A *yukata* is a lightweight cotton robe.
5. Issa is alluding, of course, to Bashō's *Oku no hosomichi* (Narrow Road to the Interior), the most influential volume of *haibun* ever written. All haiku poets after Bashō must wrestle with the great master's tradition in order to find their own voices.
6. "Happy One" is the literal translation of Fuku, a common Japanese nickname for toads.
7. Burning mosquitoes was the common way of dealing with them other than by using mosquito nets.
8. Issa apparently thought these verses by Tochi and Ransetsu had been written by Bashō.
9. Nobuyuki Yuasa notes that the working poor in Issa's district often sought winter work in Tokyo and were called "starlings" as they flocked along the road.
10. Visiting a bathhouse in Edo for the customary midwinter purification bath (a Shinto custom), Issa saw his fellow bathers were steeplejacks, firemen, and *yakuza*, or gangsters identifiable by their large tattoos.

11. During the popular Setsubun festival in the first week of February, the official beginning of spring, it was the custom to throw beans and chant these lines.

12. In Issa's time, I Shinshu (now Nagano Prefecture) was notorious for the "bad things" people ate: cicada pupae, bee worms, and the like.

13. Jizō is the patron god of children and travelers.

14. Same as Jizō, "O" being an added honorific.

15. This poem alludes to the folk saying *"Tonde hi ni iru natsu no mushi"* (Summer bugs plunge into fire of their own volition; a fool hunts for his fortune).

Index of first lines

About the Translator and the Artist

SAM HAMILL is the author of more than thirty books of poetry, translations, and essays, including *Only Companion: Japanese Poems of Love and Longing*, *The Erotic Spirit*, *Destination Zero: Poems 1970–1995*, and (with Keiko Matsui Gibson) *River of Stars: Selected Poems of Yosano Akiko*. He has been awarded fellowships from the National Endowment for the Arts, the Guggenheim Foundation, the Japan–U.S. Friendship Commission, the Lila Wallace–Reader's Digest Foundation, and the Andrew Mellon Foundation.

KAJI ASO is a widely respected artist whose works are listed in Japan as National Property. He teaches art, art history, and Asian culture at the Kaji Aso Studio and the Museum of Fine Arts in Boston.

SHAMBHALA CENTAUR EDITIONS are named for a classical modern typeface designed by the eminent American typographer Bruce Rogers. Modeled on a fifteenth-century Roman type, Centaur was originally an exclusive titling font for the Metropolitan Museum of Art, New York. The first book in which it appeared was Maurice de Guérin's *The Centaur*, printed in 1915.

Originally, Centaur type was available only for handset books printed on letterpress. Its elegance and clarity make it the typeface of choice for Shambhala Centaur Editions, which include outstanding classics of the world's literary and spiritual traditions.

Shambhala Centaur Editions

AFTER IKKYU AND OTHER POEMS
by Jim Harrison

BOOK OF THE HEART
Embracing the Tao
by Loy Ching-Yuen
Translated by Trevor Carolan and Bella Chen

DEWDROPS ON A LOTUS LEAF
Zen Poems of Ryokan
Translated by John Stevens

FOUR HUTS
Asian Writings on the Simple Life
Translated by Burton Watson

LOOK! THIS IS LOVE!
Poems of Rumi
Translated by Annemarie Schimmel

ONLY COMPANION
Japanese Poems of Love and Longing
Translated by Sam Hamill

PRAYER OF THE HEART
Writings from the Philokalia
   Compiled by Saint Nikodimus of the Holy Mountain
   and Saint Makarios of Corinth
   Translated by G. E. H. Palmer, Philip Sherrard, and
   Kallistos Ware

RIVER OF STARS
Selected Poems of Yosano Akiko
   Translated by Sam Hamill and Keiko Matsui Gibson

SONGS OF THE SONS AND DAUGHTERS
OF THE BUDDHA
   Translated by Andrew Schelling and Anne Waldman

A TOUCH OF GRACE
Songs of Kabir
   Translated by Linda Hess and Shukdev Singh

WILD WAYS
The Zen Poems of Ikkyu
   Translated by John Stevens